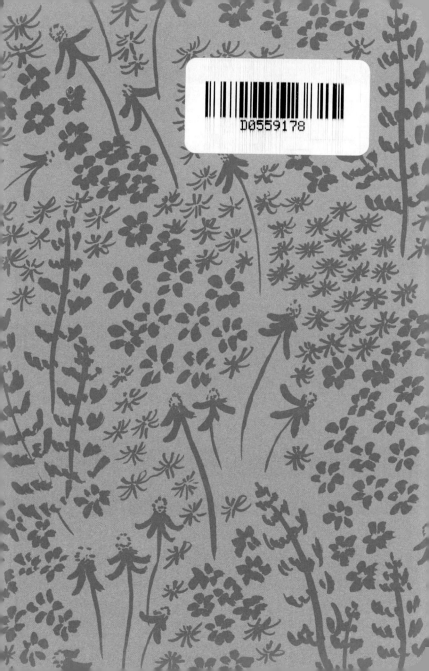

The Gardener Says

Also available in the
Words of Wisdom series:

The Architect Says
Laura S. Dushkes

The Designer Says
Sara Bader

The Filmmaker Says
Jamie Thompson Stern

The Chef Says
Nach Waxman and Matt Sartwell

The Musician Says
Benedetta LoBalbo

The Inventor Says
Kevin Lippert

The Writer Says
Kevin Lippert

the GARDENER *says*

Quotes, Quips, and Words of Wisdom

compiled and edited by Nina Pick

Princeton Architectural Press, New York

My favorite garden is my mother's. It grows chaotically, always on the brink of overflowing. The house, located near the center of town, has only a small yard, yet the garden is full of wildness. The bright flowers attract bees and hummingbirds. The soil, nourished with compost, is alive with happy-looking worms. Following the principles of companion planting, the garden contains roses growing incongruously next to tomatoes, beans next to nasturtiums, squash next to morning glories. It also has occasional visitors—robins and rabbits, and once even a bobcat, down from the mountain.

What I love most about her garden, though, is her affection for it. The garden can be a source of stress, certainly—how soon to plant in the early spring, when to prune in fall, how to find time for weeding in the middle of a busy week—but primarily it gives her joy. Abundant, gratuitous, overwhelming joy. She's beaming when I catch her standing among the pole beans in the summer, and she's beaming just reading the seed catalogues in the middle of winter. Like the chickadees and the hummingbirds and the worms and the rabbits, when she's in the garden she looks as if she's perfectly situated in the most beautiful place in the universe.

The writers and gardeners quoted in this volume delight in all of gardening's many moods and phases. They name both the joys and challenges: the exhaustion at the end of a long day's work, the amazement at watching a seedling sprout, the peace and happiness of time spent in reverie on a quiet bench. As they celebrate the garden's mysteries, in prose and poetry, with humor and wonder and humility, their language itself seems to be a kind of blossoming. "Thank you zinnia, and gooseberry, rudbeckia / and pawpaw, Ashmead's kernel, cockscomb / and scarlet runner, feverfew and lemonbalm; / thank you knitbone and sweetgrass and sunchoke… / good lord please give me a minute," writes poet Ross Gay, his gratitude fecund and spilling over. Their words show gardening and writing as intertwined creative processes. As Michael Pollan says, "Writing and gardening, these two ways of rendering the world in rows, have a great deal in common." Or, as Elizabeth Lawrence describes, "Gardening, reading about gardening, and writing about gardening are all one; no one can garden alone."

The authors in this book remind us that a garden is a place of community, a place of worship, a place of work that is aligned not with capitalism but with the greater creative work of nature. As Robin Wall Kimmerer, author of *Braiding Sweetgrass: Indigenous Wisdom, Scientific Knowledge, and the Teaching of Plants*, writes, "A garden is a nursery for nurturing connection, the soil for cultivation of practical reverence." Michelle Obama, who grew the largest vegetable garden ever planted on the White House lawn, similarly emphasizes that children need to garden so that they can learn where their food comes from and see that it doesn't come into being shrink-wrapped at the grocery store but is the result of the human-earth relationship. The act, and the art, of gardening restores us to our senses, both literally and figuratively; it propels us away from our screens and into the world.

One of my favorite quotes in this compilation of favorite quotes is farmer-poet Wendell Berry's "I can think of no better form of personal involvement in the cure of the environment than that of gardening." Gardening promotes an ecological healing that affects both the earth and the gardener. With our hands in the dirt, we attain a kind of intimacy with place. We are located on and in the earth, participants in its process of creation. We come into right relation with nature, giving it our care and attention; in turn, and seemingly miraculously, the earth blossoms.

Gardening is a form of attention, a tending to the wonders all around us. Writer Philip Simmons, who upon facing death from ALS at the age of thirty-five committed to documenting the miracles of daily life, reminds us, "Anyone who's spent time on her knees in a berry patch or flower bed comes to see this attention to small things as a form of prayer, a way of vanishing, for one sweet hour, into whatever crumb of creation we are privileged to take into our hands." As Simmons emphasizes, a garden shows us how to see. And, as *The Secret Garden* author Frances Hodgson Burnett says, "If you look the right way, you can see that the whole world is a garden." The lessons learned in a garden—care, hard work, patience, faith—teach us how to be good citizens, good friends and neighbors and lovers, good members of our human communities as well as of the more-than-human world.

My hope is that this book will invite you to participate in gardening in any form that is right for you—from enjoying a public garden in quiet contemplation to placing a houseplant on your windowsill, from planting a phrase of daffodils to entire paragraphs of sweet peas. May you be nurtured by these garden quotes and by your own wild gardens, wherever you may find them.

If you look the right way, you can see that the whole world is a garden.

Frances Hodgson Burnett (1849–1924)

EVERYBODY HAS AN OPINION ABOUT GARDENING.

Troy Scott-Smith (1971–)

Good gardening is very simple, really. You just have to learn to think like a plant.

Barbara Damrosch (1942–)

Anyone who's spent time
on her knees in a berry patch
or flower bed comes to see
this attention to small
things as a form of prayer,
a way of vanishing, for
one sweet hour, into
whatever crumb of creation
we are privileged to take
into our hands.

Philip Simmons (1957–2002)

To forget how to dig the earth and tend the soil is to forget ourselves.

Mahatma Gandhi (1869–1948)

A garden should feel like a walk in the woods.

Dan Kiley (1912–2004)

IN THE SPRING, AT THE END OF THE DAY, YOU SHOULD SMELL LIKE DIRT.

Margaret Atwood (1939–)

A garden is
a grand teacher.
It teaches patience
and careful
watchfulness;
it teaches industry
and thrift;
above all it teaches
entire trust.

Gertrude Jekyll (1843–1932)

SOMETIMES A TREE TELLS YOU MORE THAN CAN BE READ IN BOOKS.

C. G. Jung (1875–1961)

Flowers always make people better, happier, and more helpful; they are sunshine, food, and medicine for the soul.

Luther Burbank (1849–1926)

Earth laughs in flowers.

Ralph Waldo Emerson (1803–82)

The great thing is
not to be timid
in your gardening,
whether it's colors,
shapes, juxtapositions,
or the contents
themselves.
Splash around
and enjoy yourself.

Christopher Lloyd (1921–2006)

There can be no other occupation like gardening in which, if you were to creep up behind someone at their work, you would find them smiling.

Mirabel Osler (1925–2016)

If you would be happy all your life, plant a garden.

Nan Fairbrother (1913–71)

Green fingers are the extensions of a verdant heart. A good garden cannot be made by somebody who has not developed the capacity to know and to love growing things.

Russell Page (1906–85)

I CAN THINK OF NO BETTER FORM OF PERSONAL INVOLVEMENT IN THE CURE OF THE ENVIRONMENT THAN THAT OF GARDENING.

Wendell Berry (1934–)

Earth has no sorrow that earth cannot heal.

John Muir (1838–1914)

IN OUR GARDENS WE WANT PLANTS, BY THEIR STRUCTURE AND POETRY, TO SUGGEST THE FINE MELANCHOLY WE EXPECT IN NATURE.

Thomas Church (1902–78)

I want death to find me planting my cabbages.

Michel de Montaigne (1533–92)

Behold this compost! behold it well!

Walt Whitman (1819–92)

LIFE INTO DEATH INTO LIFE.

Alan Chadwick (1909–80)

The love of dirt is one of the earliest of passions, as it is the latest.... So long as we are dirty, we are pure.

Charles Dudley Warner (1829–1900)

If [a gardener] were to go to the garden of Eden, he would sniff intoxicatedly and say, "There's humus here, by God!"

Karel Čapek (1890–1938)

"More, more, more"
is my gardening motto.
If growing a single
kind of daylily is one
of life's good things,
then growing
thirty, forty, or even
a hundred of them
is one of life's
even better things.

Allen Lacy (1935–2015)

I've never seen a gardener who hasn't room for one more plant.

Lee May (1941–2014)

The great majority of the flowers in my garden are in their present places because they have personally informed me, in the clearest possible tones, that this is where they wish to be.

Beverley Nichols (1898–1983)

LET PLANTS CHOOSE THEIR DESTINIES.

Nancy Lawson (1970–)

A firm resolution should be made to purchase only a plant for a place, and never to come home wondering where to place a plant.

Graham Stuart Thomas (1909–2003)

NO PLANT GOES INTO MY GARDEN UNLESS A PLACE IS READY TO RECEIVE IT IN WHICH EVERYTHING NEEDFUL FOR ITS PROSPERITY AND SAFETY HAS BEEN PROVIDED.

Herbert Durand (1859–1944)

PLANTS WANT TO GROW; THEY ARE ON YOUR SIDE AS LONG AS YOU ARE REASONABLY SENSIBLE.

Anne Wareham (1959–)

All we have to do is create the right environment for growth.

Dan Pearson (1964–)

Patience is a lazy gardener's best friend.

Mara Grey (1949–)

GARDENING IS THE SLOWEST OF THE PERFORMING ARTS.

Mac Griswold (1942–)

Any gardening is better than none, but some ways of gardening are better than others.

Robin Lane Fox (1946–)

Gardens are diverse as the people who make them.

Ann Lovejoy (*1951–*)

Every time I imagine a garden
in an architectural setting,
it turns into a magical place.
I think of gardens I have seen,
that I believe I have seen,
that I long to see, surrounded
by simple walls, columns,
arcades, or the facades of
buildings—sheltered places
of great intimacy where
I want to stay for a long time.

Peter Zumthor (1943–)

A natural garden calls for paths, whether hard or soft, to allow the user to wander and make discoveries, so that all is not revealed at first glance.

John Brookes (1933–2018)

A LAWN IS NATURE UNDER TOTALITARIAN RULE.

Michael Pollan (1955–)

LEARN GARDENING FROM THE WILDERNESS OUTSIDE THE GARDEN GATE.

Wendy Johnson (1947–)

There are two seasonal
diversions that can
ease the bite of any winter.
One is the January thaw.
The other is the seed
catalogues.

Hal Borland (1900–78)

From December to March, there are for many of us three gardens—the garden outdoors, the garden of pots and bowls in the house, and the garden of the mind's eye.

Katherine S. White (1892–1977)

Acts of creation are ordinarily
reserved for gods and poets,
but humbler folk may circumvent
this restriction if they know how.
To plant a pine, for example,
one need be neither god nor poet;
one need only own a shovel.

Aldo Leopold (*1887–1948*)

THERE ARE SO MANY
FABULOUS THINGS
ABOUT GARDENING,
AND THE BEST
IS THAT ANYONE
CAN DO IT.

C. Z. Guest (1920–2003)

IN GARDENS, BEAUTY IS A BY-PRODUCT. THE MAIN BUSINESS IS SEX AND DEATH.

Sam Llewelyn (1948–)

How I love the mixture of the beautiful and the squalid in gardening. It makes it so lifelike.

Evelyn Underhill (1875–1941)

The scent of warm soil…
is deep, rich, and sexy.
It's primal. It's earthy.
It makes you want to run
outside, get down on
hands and knees, gather
a fistful, and inhale.

Tovah Martin (1953–)

Garden writing is often very tame,
a real waste when you think how
opinionated, inquisitive, irreverent
and lascivious gardeners themselves
tend to be. Nobody talks much about
the muscular limbs, dark, swollen
buds, strip-tease trees, and unholy
beauty that have made us all
slaves of the Goddess Flora.

Ketzel Levine (1953–)

Weeds come up as easily as plants go in; there is an almost sexual relationship between plant and earth. The ecstasy is short lived, but that is the nature of ecstasy.

Hugh Johnson (1939–)

I am very busy picking up stems and stamens as the hollyhocks leave their clothes around.

Emily Dickinson (1830–86)

Gardening is akin to writing stories. No experience could have taught me more about grief or flowers, about achieving survival by going, your fingers in the ground, the limit of physical exhaustion.

Eudora Welty (1909–2001)

Gardens are the story of two things: culture and biology. Gardeners are the storytellers.

Augustus Jenkins Farmer (1966–)

IT IS NO DOUBT THAT GARDENING SPARKS OFF HAREBRAINED IDEAS.

Mirabel Osler (1925–2016)

GARDENING IS NOT A RATIONAL ACTIVITY.

Margaret Atwood (1939–)

Don't think the garden loses its ecstasy in winter. It's quiet, but the roots are down there riotous.

Rumi *(1207–73)*

Soil is the substance of transformation.

Carol Williams (1948–)

Some kids have never
seen what a real tomato
looks like off the vine.
They don't know where
a cucumber comes from.
And that really affects
the way they view food.
So a garden helps them
really get their hands dirty,
literally, and understand
the whole process of where
their food comes from.

Michelle Obama (1964–)

A garden is a nursery for nurturing connection, the soil for cultivation of practical reverence.

Robin Wall Kimmerer (1953–)

{Growing our own food}
is—in addition to being the
appropriate fulfillment of
a practical need—a sacrament,
as eating is also, by which
we enact and understand
our oneness with the Creation,
the conviviality of one body
with all bodies.

Wendell Berry (1934–)

A garden with vegetables, fruits, and flowers feeds body and soul. Grow all of them.

Andrew Weil (1942–)

IT IS NOT JUST PLANTS THAT GROW, BUT THE GARDENERS THEMSELVES.

Ken Druse (1950–)

GARDENING IS A SACRED ACT.

Fran Sorin (1953–)

Gardening involves
the incredibly complicated
alchemy of life,
involving not just plants
and animals, but
the entire cosmos and
the microcosm.

Wolf D. Storl (1942–)

One teaspoon of soil can contain more living creatures than there are people in the world.

John Robbins (1947–)

Trees could solve
the problem
if people trying
to improve things
would only
allow them to
take over.

Peter Wohlleben (1964–)

I HAVE GREAT FAITH IN A SEED.

Henry David Thoreau (1817–62)

Gardening makes sense
in a senseless world.
By extension, then, the
more gardens in the world,
the more justice,
the more *sense* is created.

Andrew Weil (1942–)

THE PLANT WORLD IS THE MIRROR OF HUMAN CONSCIENCE.

Rudolf Steiner (1861–1925)

My whole life has been spent waiting
for an epiphany, a manifestation of God's
presence, the kind of transcendent,
magical experience that lets you see our
place in the big picture. And that is
what I had with my first [compost] heap.

Bette Midler (1945–)

The view from your bedroom window should include something that blooms every spring.

Michelle Slatalla (1961–)

*Without
flowers,
I'd find life
very dismal.*

C. Z. Guest (1920–2003)

WHEN YOU BRING FLOWERS INTO YOUR VEGETABLE PATCH, BE PREPARED FOR GOOD THINGS TO HAPPEN.

Lisa Mason Ziegler (1961–)

*Thank you zinnia, and
    gooseberry, rudbeckia
and pawpaw, Ashmead's
    kernel, cockscomb
and scarlet runner, feverfew
    and lemonbalm;
thank you knitbone and
    sweetgrass and sunchoke...
good lord please give me
    a minute.*

Ross Gay (1974–)

I MUST HAVE FLOWERS, ALWAYS AND ALWAYS.

Claude Monet (*1840–1926*)

Let no one think that
real gardening is a bucolic
and meditative occupation.
It is an insatiable passion,
like everything else to
which man gives his heart.

Karel Čapek (1890–1938)

Horticultural passions are peculiar things. A mild interest in that plant or another can suddenly flame into something more nearly describable as an obsession.

Allen Lacy *(1935–2015)*

The gardener cultivates wildness, but he does so carefully and respectfully, in full recognition of its mystery.

Michael Pollan (1955–)

[A GARDEN] HAS A LIFE OF ITS OWN, AN INTRICATE, WILLFUL, SECRET LIFE.

W. S. Merwin (1927–)

Time is the essence of garden-making as a creative endeavor.

Tim Richardson (1968–)

Though I am an old man,
I am but a young gardener.

Thomas Jefferson *(1743–1826)*

Plant for the garden you will have five years from now.

Michelle Slatalla (1961–)

GARDEN AS THOUGH YOU WILL LIVE FOREVER.

William Kent (1685–1748)

*I ALWAYS
THINK OF MY SINS
WHEN I WEED.
THEY GROW APACE
IN THE SAME WAY,
AND ARE
HARDER STILL
TO GET RID OF.*

Helen Rutherford Ely (1858–1920)

No pain, no gain, and
that is why my garden
has gained so little
over the years, I guess.
To me a garden is
no place for pain.
You can find enough
of that at the office.

Henry Mitchell (1923–93)

Gardens are living creatures that we would like to be happy. Our task is to act lovingly, carefully, and protectively.

Paolo Pejrone (1941–)

PLANTS NEED LOVE.

Shawna Coronado (1966–)

The greatest delight
which the fields
and woods minister
is the suggestion
of an occult relation
between man and
the vegetable.
I am not alone and
unacknowledged.
They nod to me, and
I to them.

Ralph Waldo Emerson (1803–82)

A GARDEN IS A RELATION, WHICH IS ONE OF THE COUNTLESS REASONS WHY IT IS NEVER FINISHED.

W. S. Merwin (1927–)

AS THINKING, FEELING BEINGS, WE HAVE AN UNTAPPED POTENTIAL TO RELATE TO THE PLANT WORLD.

Judith Handelsman (1948–)

*PLANTS TALK TO US
AT ALL LEVELS,
MOLECULE TO MOLECULE,
AND SPIRIT TO SPIRIT.*

Marlene Adelmann (1955–)

Gardening, reading about gardening, and writing about gardening are all one; no one can garden alone.

Elizabeth Lawrence (1904–85)

Writing and gardening, these two ways of rendering the world in rows, have a great deal in common.

Michael Pollan (1955–)

GARDENS ARE A FORM OF AUTOBIOGRAPHY.

Sydney Eddison (1932–)

I was reared in the garden, you know.

Emily Dickinson (1830–86)

Good gardening and a quiet life seldom go hand in hand.

Christopher Lloyd (1921–2006)

GARDENING IS THE BEST THERAPY IN THE WORLD.

C. Z. Guest (1920–2003)

Gardens aren't installations, they don't need to be attractive as soon as they're completed: gardens can grow and, like all newborn creatures, they should have that rare and special privilege of being awkward and graceless.

Paolo Pejrone (1941–)

A GARDEN THAT IS DESIGNED ONLY TO LOOK PRETTY BARELY SKIMS THE SURFACE OF WHAT LANDSCAPES CAN OFFER.

Toby Hemenway (1952–2016)

In setting a garden we are
painting—a picture of hundreds
of feet or yards instead of
so many inches, painted with
living flowers and seen by
open daylight—so that to paint
it rightly is a debt that we owe
to the beauty of flowers and
to the light of the sun.

William Robinson (1838–1935)

All gardening is landscape painting.

William Kent *(ca. 1685–1748)*

Painting is closely related to gardening but closer still is poetry.

Robert Dash (1934–2013)

METHINKS MY OWN SOUL MUST BE A BRIGHT INVISIBLE GREEN.

Henry David Thoreau (1817–62)

I try for beauty and harmony everywhere, and especially for harmony of color.

Gertrude Jekyll (1843–1932)

BLUE, BLUE,
BLUE, MELTING,
CERULEAN,
ALTOGETHER
EXQUISITE AND
DESIRABLE.

Reginald Farrer (1880–1920)

I cannot help hoping that
the great ghostly barn-owl
will sweep silently across
a pale garden, next summer,
in the twilight—the pale
garden that I am now planting,
under the first flakes of snow.

Vita Sackville-West (1892–1962)

My garden is my most beautiful masterpiece.

Claude Monet *(1840–1926)*

Precisely because it is an archetype the garden must be subject to constant reinterpretation.

J. B. Jackson (1909–96)

THE BEST GARDEN DESIGNERS TAKE RISKS.

James van Sweden *(1935–2013)*

DESIGN...THE SPACE IN CONSIDERATION OF CONTEMPORARY ART.

Mirei Shigemori (1896–1975)

It's not what you see, but what you see in it.

Piet Oudolf (1944–)

ROSES... COME TO US LADEN WITH STORIES.

Jennifer Potter (1949–)

The history of roses is the history of humanity.

J. H. Nicholas (1875–1937)

Thank goodness violets are some of the first flowers to blossom in spring.

Tovah Martin (1953–)

There is a kind of *sorcery* to tulips.

Mirabel Osler (1925–2016)

AS LONG AS ONE HAS A GARDEN, ONE HAS A FUTURE; AND AS LONG AS ONE HAS A FUTURE ONE IS ALIVE.

Frances Hodgson Burnett (1849–1924)

On the last day of the world
I would want to plant a tree.

W. S. Merwin *(1927–)*

When I say to people
my primary focus
at Sissinghurst is
romance and beauty,
they are shocked and
seem unbelieving.
Folk generally consider
gardens to be about
plants and horticulture.

Troy Scott-Smith (1971–)

Surely the business of the blue garden is to be beautiful first, as well as to be blue. My own idea is that it should be beautiful first, and then just as blue as may be consistent with its best possible beauty.

Gertrude Jekyll (1843–1932)

GARDENS... ARE OFTEN
BEAUTIFUL, VITAL, AND EXCITING:
AND PERHAPS THEY OWE THIS
TO THE DELICATE SYNTHESIS
BETWEEN FRAGILITY AND STRENGTH,
AND THE EVER RARER FUSION
BETWEEN LIGHTNESS AND SOLIDITY,
BETWEEN THE MOMENT IN TIME
AND THE ABSOLUTE.

Paolo Pejrone (1941–)

I would say that people who try to do research on the garden have to very seriously study the way of tea.

Mirei Shigemori (1896–1975)

A vegetable garden
[is] a place where if you
can't say "I love you"
out loud, you can say it
in seeds.

Robin Wall Kimmerer (1953–)

The pleasure of owning a fine plant is not complete until it has been given to friends.

Peter Smithers (1913–2006)

THERE'S NOTHING LIKE NATURE TO TEACH GARDEN DESIGN.

Lee May (1941–2014)

THE BEST OF ALL GREEN GARDENERS IS MOTHER NATURE.

Pat Welsh (1929–)

Where the beautiful parts of nature are justly imitated in gardens, they will always be approved by judicious persons, let the taste of gardening alter as it will.

Philip Miller (1691–1771)

No house or garden is complete without shrubs.

C. Z. Guest (1920–2003)

THE LESSON I HAVE
THOROUGHLY LEARNED,
AND WISH TO PASS ON
TO OTHERS, IS TO KNOW
THE ENDURING HAPPINESS
THAT THE LOVE OF A
GARDEN GIVES.

Gertrude Jekyll (*1843–1932*)

Wherever humans garden magnificently, there are magnificent heartbreaks.

Henry Mitchell (1923–93)

It came to me while picking beans, the secret of happiness.

Robin Wall Kimmerer (1953–)

The right tomato can move you to tears.

Craig LeHoullier (1956–)

A garden is a way of living with nature, as we live with those we love.

Cassandra Danz (1942–2002)

Emotional ties to plants are binding.

Lee May *(1941–2014)*

It was not till I experimented with seeds plucked straight from a growing plant that I had my first success—the first thrill of creation—the taste of blood. This, surely, must be akin to the pride of paternity.

Beverley Nichols (1898–1983)

THE SOONER THE GARDENER LOSES CERTAIN KINDS OF INNOCENCE THE BETTER.

Henry Mitchell (1923–93)

We will gladly send the management
a jar of our wife's green-tomato pickle
from last summer's crop—dark green,
spicy, delicious, costlier than pearls
when you consider the overhead.

E. B. White (1899–1985)

I...GROW PERENNIALS BECAUSE I'M CHEAP.

Cassandra Danz (1947–2002)

When your garden is finished
I hope it will be more beautiful
than you had anticipated,
require less care than you expected,
and have cost only a little more
than you had planned.

Thomas Church (1902–78)

I SHALL NEVER
HAVE THE GARDEN
I HAVE IN MY
MIND, BUT THAT
FOR ME IS THE
JOY OF IT;
CERTAIN THINGS
CAN NEVER BE
REALIZED AND SO
ALL THE MORE
REASON TO
ATTEMPT THEM.

Jamaica Kincaid (1949–)

In the garden we can experience the connectedness and trust in change— and even death—because there is a continuum; there are no final endings.

Elizabeth Murray (1953–)

GARDENERS HAVE TO BELIEVE THAT THE DEAD WILL REINCARNATE.

Mirabel Osler (1925–2016)

I feel very strongly in the sort of planting that I do, that you feel the changes all the time. It is a changing beauty: from beauty into beauty.

Piet Oudolf (1944–)

GARDENING IS AN INSTRUMENT OF GRACE.

May Sarton (1912–95)

Give me juicy autumnal fruit ripe and red from the orchard.

Walt Whitman (1819–92)

Spare us the beauty of fruit-trees.

H. D. (1886–1961)

The whole starry heaven is involved in the growth of plants.

Rudolf Steiner (1861–1925)

In the name of the Bee—
And of the Butterfly—
And of the Breeze—Amen.

Emily Dickinson (1830–86)

May our heart's garden of awakening bloom with hundreds of flowers.

Thích Nhất Hạnh (1926–)

I would like to thank Jan Cigliano Hartman for sharing her idea for *The Gardener Says* and for her enthusiastic support of the project; all the writers whose inspiring words appear in this book; the Horticultural Society of New York for the use of its wonderful library; the entire staff of Princeton Architectural Press (with a special thank you to designer Ben English); and my mother, my favorite gardener.

Nina Pick

Published by
Princeton Architectural Press
A McEvoy Group company
202 Warren Street, Hudson, NY 12534
www.papress.com

Princeton Architectural Press is a
leading publisher in architecture, design,
photography, landscape, and visual culture.
We create fine books and stationery of
unsurpassed quality and production
values. With more than one thousand titles
published, we find design everywhere
and in the most unlikely places.

Editor: Nina Pick
Designer: Benjamin English
Endpapers: Anita Sidler

Special thanks to: Paula Baver, Janet Behning,
Abby Bussel, Jan Cigliano Hartman,
Susan Hershberg, Kristen Hewitt, Lia Hunt,
Valerie Kamen, Jennifer Lippert, Sara McKay,
Parker Menzimer, Eliana Miller, Wes Seeley,
Rob Shaeffer, Sara Stemen, Marisa Tesoro,
Paul Wagner, and Joseph Weston
of Princeton Architectural Press
—Kevin C. Lippert, publisher

Library of Congress Cataloging-
in-Publication Data:
Names: Pick, Nina, compiler, editor.
Title: The gardener says : quotes, quips,
    and words of wisdom / compiled & edited
    by Nina Pick.
Description: First edition. | New York :
    Princeton Architectural Press, [2019] |
    Includes index.
Identifiers: LCCN 2018023973 |
    ISBN 9781616897765
Subjects: LCSH: Gardening—Quotations,
    maxims, etc.
Classification: LCC SB455 .G352 2019 |
    DDC 635—dc23
LC record available at https://lccn.loc
    .gov/2018023973

BUT OF COURSE! WHEN THE IMPULSE TO GARDEN STRIKES, YOU GARDEN!

Susan Brownmiller (1935–)